INTRODUCTION

KT-524-858

The internet can be a wonderful thing.
It allows you to play games, watch film trailers,
talk to people all over the world and watch
many, many videos of baby animals falling over.

But, just like in your everyday, offline life,
you may come across people who are rude and
unpleasant. Some people even use the internet to
commit crimes.

This book is full of tips on how to use the
internet safely, and how to deal with people who
behave badly there. There are also examples of
good things you can do online: it's not *all* bad news.

There's no need to be scared. If you take a
few precautions and approach the internet
with caution as well as curiosity, it can be an
incredible playground for your brain.

CONTENTS

USBORNE
STAYING
SAFE
ONLINE

Louie Stowell

Designed & illustrated by Nancy Leschnikoff

Expert advice from: Jennifer Perry,
CEO of Digital-Trust

Edited by Felicity Brooks

Photographs on page 86: skateboarder ©Daniel Milchev/Getty Images;
bearded man © Daniel Berehulak / Staff/Getty Images; tardigrade ©Eraxion/
iStock/Thinkstock; kitten ©Martin Poole/DigitalVision/Thinkstock;
baby turtle ©italiansight/ iStock/Thinkstock

Usborne Publishing Ltd., 83-85 Saffron Hill, London, EC1N 8RT, England.
Printed in UK. This edition first published in 2016 www.usborne.com
Copyright © 2016 Usborne Publishing Ltd.
The name Usborne and the devices ♀ ⊕ are Trade Marks of Usborne Publishing Ltd.

2

6208335

What the internet feels like when everything's going smoothly.

8

This chapter takes you through some internet safety basics. But first...

WHAT IS THE INTERNET?

The internet is a collection of computers — billions of them — that are connected together by cables or by signals flying through the air.

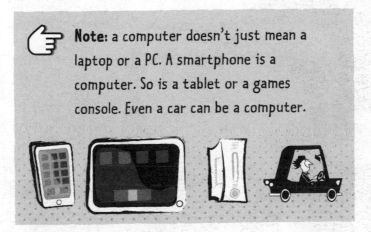

Note: a computer doesn't just mean a laptop or a PC. A smartphone is a computer. So is a tablet or a games console. Even a car can be a computer.

The internet allows computers (and the people using them) to share information.

At the most basic level, the internet does two things:

1. Sends your information from your device out into the world.

2. Brings information from other people to your device.

(If you want to know more about the technical side of things, you'll find links at the Usborne Quicklinks website — see page 138 for details.)

SO, WHY IS THE INTERNET DANGEROUS?

When your phone (or any device) is connected to the internet, you might find yourself sharing more than you bargained for (such as your money) or receiving things you really didn't want (such as viruses, or nasty messages).

Here are some risks of being online:

1. Cyberbullies: these are just like normal bullies, only online. Cyberbullies can be every bit as hurtful and scary as offline ones, and you can't just go home and shut your door against them.

You'll find tips on how to deal with cyberbullies later in the book.

Billy goats suck LOL!

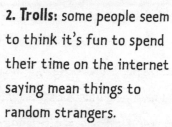

2. Trolls: some people seem to think it's fun to spend their time on the internet saying mean things to random strangers.

Internet trolls should mostly be pitied, as it's a real waste of time, and probably means they don't have very good social skills. But it's important to know how to deal with a troll when you come across one. (More on this later.)

3. Hacked accounts: if someone gets hold of your passwords they can post things pretending to be you — embarrassing things or things that will get you into trouble. Sometimes when friends argue, this is something someone might do when feeling angry, without thinking about how it might make someone else feel.

4. Harmful words and images: people put some upsetting things online, from violent images and hateful posts encouraging you to harm people, to images and videos that aren't bad in themselves, but aren't suitable for kids. You'll find tips on how to avoid things like this in chapters 8 and 9.

5. Viruses: Viruses are computer programs designed to "infect" your computer and change how it works. They make your phone, tablet or laptop stop working properly, and you might even have to buy a new phone AND lose all your pictures and contacts. Viruses can also be used to steal information, such as bank details, so they are bad news all round.

We're going to eat your photos, mwahahaha!

6. Criminals: unfortunately, there are people out there who use the internet to steal and commit other, even more serious, crimes. Some of these criminals are hackers: people with a lot of computer knowledge who access your device without permission, via the internet.

NOT ALL HACKERS ARE BAD

Not all hackers do harm. Some just want to prove they *can* sneak into your computer — it's like a dare to them. Others use their hacking skills to find out information that companies or governments don't want people to know, and share it with the world. (That could be bad or good, depending on your point of view.)

BASIC SAFETY TIPS

Even when you know that, in theory, there are dangers online, it's easy to have a false sense of security: a phone feels like a very private thing, nestled in your pocket. But when you're connected to the internet, that's like having a door in your pocket leading to the rest of the world.

Here are some easy ways to make sure that door remains guarded... and that you stay safe.

CREATING STRONG PASSWORDS

One way to help protect you from hackers and people sneaking their way into your online accounts is to make sure the passwords you use are very hard to guess.

The worst passwords are predictable ones, such as your name and birthday. The best are random strings of letters, numbers and symbols.

The trouble with secure passwords is they're often not very memorable.

Obviously, *you* need to be able to remember them to access your accounts. One good way to do this is to use a password manager, which is a computer program that creates and stores passwords for you. No site is 100% safe from hackers, but password manager websites are more secure than most sites.

 Tip: never enter your password when someone else can see what you're typing.

SECRET CODES

If you don't want to use a password manager, you could invent a code that will help you create passwords that are hard for other people to guess, but easy for you to remember. For example:

- Take the first letter of the website or app that you're using. Make this uppercase.

- Add up all the numbers of your birthdate.

- Add a symbol (something other than !, as people use that one a lot in passwords).

- End with the first three letters of the website you're using, backwards and lowercase.

Or you could create your own code. Whatever you do, don't write down your passwords, as it's very easy to lose a notebook or a piece of paper. Don't re-use passwords, either, as if someone finds out your password once, they can get everywhere.

AN EXTRA STEP

You can make online accounts, such as your email and social networking sites, safer by using something called "two-step authentication". This just means that when you log in to a site from an unusual place, such as a friend's laptop, it will ask you to go through an extra step — typing in a number that will be texted to your mobile phone — before you're allowed in.

Go to the help page for each website or app, and type in "two-step authentication" to find out how to set it up.

AVOIDING VIRUSES

It's important to download anti-virus software for any computers you have, whether it's a phone, tablet, laptop or anything else that you connect to the internet. This will probably cost money so talk to your parents about it. You can usually get one that covers all your devices.

As well as downloading anti-virus software, there are things to *avoid* downloading. Videos, pictures or music can infect your phone, as can clicking on links in emails.

BACK UP AND UPDATE

To keep your photos, schoolwork and other files safe, in case something bad happens to your phone or computer, it's important to back up your device. You can do this using "cloud computing" — a type of shared storage involving lots of computers — or using an external hard drive. It's also very important to download any security updates that appear in your settings on your phone or computer.

 Downloading security updates can help protect you against viruses, in addition to anti-virus software.

SAFETY BASICS: A QUIZ

1. Which of these is a common risk of being online?

a) Ruptured appendix

b) Cyberbullies

c) Cybermen

d) Duck attacks

2. Which of these is a strong password?

a) Your birthday

b) Your name

c) A jumble of letters, symbols and numbers

d) The word "password"

3. Why should you back up and update your devices?

a) So you don't lose your photos and other files if your computer goes wrong

b) To make your phone battery last longer

c) To prevent rust

d) Because it's deeply enjoyable

4. A troll is...

a) The natural enemy of a billy goat

b) Someone who says horrible things on the internet

c) A type of fish

d) A piece of self-assembly furniture from a Swedish shop

5. What is two-step authentication?

a) An 18th Century dance

b) Something hackers use to break into government computers

c) Fake ID underage teenagers use to get into clubs

d) A log-on process that keeps your accounts safer

6. You get an email from someone you don't recognize, telling you that you've won a load of money. Should you...

a) Delete it, it's probably spam

b) Reply immediately, giving them your bank account details.

c) Forward it to all your friends

d) Click on the link in the email. Money! Woo!

ANSWERS: 1 = b 2 = c 3 = a 4 = b 5 = d 6 = a

If you got more than one answer wrong, read this chapter again — carefully.

In case the warnings and safety tips in this book start to make you feel as though the internet is a dark place, here's a reminder of something good about the internet. You'll find these at the end of each chapter.

Reasons to love the internet #1:
IT'S FREE

Yes, it costs money to have a phone plan, or an internet connection, but the internet itself costs nothing to use.

Tim Berners Lee, the British inventor of the World Wide Web*, originally created it so that scientists could share information about their experiments. He didn't ask anyone for any money for his invention: it was his gift to the world.

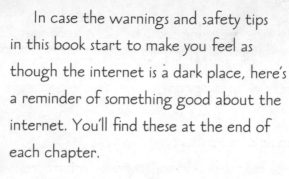

To everyone,
love from
Tim xx

WEB

*That's the part of the internet that allows people to access websites.

FRIENDSHIPS & SOCIAL MEDIA

When you're using social media it's very easy to overshare and regret it later. This chapter gives tips on how to take control of what you share, and who you share it with.

People often talk about "real life" as though it's separate from life on the internet. But if someone is mean to you online, it can hurt just as much as if they do it to your face, or if someone's kind and supportive, you can still get a warm glow, knowing that your friends are there for you. Your words and the pictures you post online matter, and can have a big effect on your life and other people's — both good and bad.

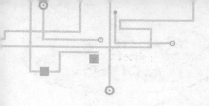

WHAT IS SOCIAL MEDIA?

Websites and apps that allow you to share photos, videos or text posts with friends (and strangers) are often known as social media, or social networks. This includes sites such as Facebook, WhatsApp and Instagram, but the chat function in an online game is also a type of social media.

YOUR SECRET IDENTITY

On sites where your posts are public and you don't have to "friend" people, don't use your real name, or give away personal information such as where you live, or your birthday. (If the site needs to know your age, give a birthday that's the same year and month as yours, but not the same day.)

On most sites, you'll need to pick a screen name. Here are a few ideas for names that don't give too much away, but still reflect your personality:

Should I be Sailor Moon Potter? Aveline Cheesesnacks? Darth Ripley?

- Your favourite book character

- A completely made-up word that you think sounds funny

- A computer game character

- A name based on a private joke between you and a friend

WHO SEES WHAT?

Most social networks give you different options about who can see what you share, such as making your posts "friends only". If in doubt, go for the highest possible privacy setting.

Sometimes, it's not very obvious how to do this, so have a look at the help page, or google "how to increase my privacy settings", for whichever site or app you're using.

One thing to bear in mind is that your friends might not be as careful as you. So if you're posting something on someone else's profile or wall, their settings might mean that your post is visible to lots of people, even if your privacy settings are high.

 Privacy tip
Usually, if you don't do anything about it, your social networking privacy settings won't be very safe. Often, the default (automatic) settings mean your posts are public.

WHAT'S SAFE TO POST?

There are some things that you should never post. Some of these things are pretty obvious: for example, your phone number; your home address; your bank account details, or where you hide the spare key to your house.

But some things aren't so clear cut. You might post something about a football match you've just won and, without realizing it, give away a clue to what school you go to, or where you live.

On my way back from winning the match. So glad it's only a five minute walk. I am EXHAUSTED!

Try not to give anything away like this — someone could easily put together a 'map' of your life and work out where you go each day. While this *probably* won't lead to you being kidnapped by an international criminal ring, it's better to be safe than sorry, and not post clues about your location.

27

SPEAKING OF LOCATION...

Make sure that you're not giving away details of where you live and spend time by posting photos of your house or your school. Also, double-check the site you're posting on doesn't automatically tag your location.

 Privacy tip
You can turn off 'Location Services' in your phone's settings so that your location is never given away. You might have to do this for each individual app on your phone, too.

ONLY ADD REAL FRIENDS

On sites where you can add people as friends, make sure you only accept requests from people you know in real life, not friends of friends (who they might not know in real life). Adding someone as a friend usually means they can see your photos and your posts — it's a little like inviting them into your house to go through your stuff. Don't worry about seeming rude. If a stranger sends you a friend request, it's your right to ignore it and keep yourself safe.

QUALITY, NOT QUANTITY

Sometimes it can feel as though everyone has more friends or followers than you on social media. But there's no point being connected to a million people if you only ever actually talk to ten of them. Try to think about who you actually want to share things with, and only add them. Having too many connections on social media can make it feel like a chore, not fun.

I'm behind on my LIKES.

I don't even know *what* I like any more.

DO I REALLY WANT TO SHARE THIS?

It's easy to post something that you regret moments (or weeks, or years) later. So before you post, try to stop and think. Ask yourself...

- Would you mind if your nan/best friend/worst enemy saw it? (Things online can travel much further than you mean them to.)

- If you're writing about someone else, is it something you'd say to their face? (See above)

- If you became famous, how would you feel if that post resurfaced on the news?

- Are you going to end up worrying about your post afterwards? If yes, is it worth the worry?

Prime Minister, any comments on that time you ate a crayon?

Wish I'd never posted that picture of me as a kid.

BAD SCIENCE AND OTHER LIES

On many sites, you can share posts that other people have made. Helping people share their thoughts can be a really nice thing to do. But not always — for example if the post you share is made-up nonsense passed off as 'fact', or if it's a mean rumour about someone.

You can do your part to make the online world better by *not* sharing things like that.

DID YOU KNOW?
RUBBING LEMON JUICE ON YOUR HANDS CAN CURE CANCER!

The internet is full of fake cures for real diseases. Spreading bad science like this helps make the world a stupider place, and can give very ill people false hope.

DON'T BELIEVE THE HYPE

Chatting to your friends online can be great. But even your very best friends can make you unhappy if you don't bear one important thing in mind:

People aren't always as happy, popular or successful as they say there are on the internet.

OMG! I'm so tired after last night's amazing party, it's hard being this popular...

Although people do complain online and talk about the bad stuff in their lives, they often edit what they say in a way that makes them look good. They post flattering photos and talk about parties they're going to... or they might complain in a way that's actually more like showing off.

So, for your own mental wellbeing, remember that people aren't telling the whole truth all the time. If you see things that make you unhappy — perhaps photos of a party you weren't invited to — try to remember that photographs don't tell the whole truth...

Is actually really bored and would rather be at home.

Just had a horrible argument with her parents on the phone and is grounded after tonight.

Is worried that he just said something stupid.

ANTI-SOCIAL NETWORK

Another social media pitfall is spending so much time talking about what you're doing, that you don't get to enjoy it in the moment. Sometimes, it's better to put away your phone and, instead of capturing the moment, just enjoy it.

SOMETHING TO THINK ABOUT

With any free social network, ask yourself what the company who runs it is getting out of it. It's likely, when a service is free, that YOU are the product. That is, the company might be selling your information, or bombarding you with adverts.

ON THE INTERNET, NOBODY KNOWS YOU'RE A DOG.

There's an old cartoon that shows a dog sitting next to a computer, with the caption: "On the internet, nobody knows you're a dog."

Although there aren't actually any canines chatting online, it's true that you can pretend to be people you're not on the internet.

Sometimes, play-acting is the whole point. For example, in an online game, you might pretend to be an elf or a robot or a soldier or whatever your character is.

Sometimes, though, people create fake identities in order to harm other people. Bullies, and adults who want to harm children, do this sometimes.

For an adult who wants to harm children, pretending to be a child or a teenager online means they have a better chance of getting hold of personal information. (There's more about this, and how to protect yourself against bad people like this, in chapter 9.)

The best way to guard against fakes like this is fairly simple...

NEVER, EVER GIVE OUT PERSONAL INFORMATION ONLINE.

Even if you *are* certain you're talking to a good friend, posting things like your address or phone number is a bad idea.

MEETING UP

Some people you meet online will want to meet up in the flesh. This is very risky. Talk to your parents or carers if someone asks you to do this.

It can sometimes be OK to meet up with people as long as you go with a trusted adult, and you're meeting somewhere public. In most cases, though, it's best to say no if someone asks you to meet them.

BLOCK AND REPORT

If someone is saying inappropriate things to you on a social network, or pestering you in any way, you can block and report them on most social media sites and apps. You should tell a trusted adult about it, too. If you don't have an adult you feel comfortable talking to, there are websites and helplines where you can get advice.

(Chapter 5 goes into more detail about how to deal with trolls and cyberbullies. Chapter 9 deals with the harmful adults you might encounter online.)

SOCIAL NETWORKING TOP TEN SAFETY TIPS

1.
Never share your password, not even with friends.

2. Don't sign up to sites with an age limit if you're not old enough.

3. Never leave yourself logged in to social networks on any device that you're not currently using.

4. Think carefully about what you post.

5.
If you see something worrying or upsetting, tell a trusted adult.

6. Check your privacy settings regularly. Sometimes, sites can change the automatic settings without you realizing.

7. Don't give out your real name on sites where strangers can talk to you.

8. Don't accept friend requests from strangers or friends of friends.

9. Never post your location, or clues about your location.

10. NEVER share personal information such as your phone number or home address.

Reasons to love the internet #2:
IT CAN HELP YOU CHANGE THE WORLD

Sometimes, people who've never met can come together on the internet and achieve amazing things.

For example, one woman used an online fundraising site to raise over £300,000 to help a pensioner who'd been mugged to buy a new home, because he was too afraid to go back to his old one.

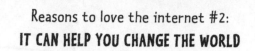

You can use social networks to help people and make your community better, whether it's sharing a picture of a lost dog so that anyone who spots it can tell the owner, or joining a campaign to save your local library.

(OR HOW NOT TO BE *THAT* PERSON ON THE INTERNET)

There are a lot of annoying people on the internet — from people who steal your ideas and take credit for them to people who are racist, sexist, or otherwise horrible. There are more subtle ways of being rude and mean online, too.

Being a good human being on the internet isn't all that different from being nice in person. But it can be easy to forget that you're talking to a person with feelings when you're typing at someone with a cartoon avatar and a made-up name.

There's a real person behind each avatar.

Aw!

YOU SUCK!

MAKING THE INTERNET BETTER FOR EVERYONE

There are no fixed rules for how you're supposed to behave online, apart from not breaking the law. Some sites have their own rules, but no one's in charge of the whole internet.

These are just some suggestions for how to treat people online. Maybe you have your own ideas about what annoys you? Add those to the 'don't do it' list, too.

WOULD YOU SAY IT TO THEIR FACE?

A good test of whether it's ok to say something online is whether you'd say it to someone's face. When you can't see the person you're talking to it can mean you go further and say worse things than you would in person.

Always remember that you ARE talking to a person.

DON'T MAKE IT PERSONAL

It's fine to be critical and have arguments, so long as you don't make it personal. Criticize what people are saying, not who they are.

 I disagree with what you just said.

 Your face is stupid and you smell of feet.

If someone asks for your opinion about something they've posted — a photo of them, or a drawing they've done, for example — then be careful about what you say, too.

Someone might ask for honest feedback but might be more sensitive than they think they are. Try to offer some positives as well as negatives, even if you hate something.

Lovely colours!

Shame about the drawing...

YOU DON'T HAVE TO JOIN IN

If a lot of people are criticizing someone at once — for example if someone has said something rude to another person —then you don't have to add to the flood of comments.

It can feel really overwhelming if loads of people are having a go at you. Even if not all the comments are angry, it might feel that way if there are dozens of them.

It was just one silly comment, please can you all stop?

WHEN THINGS COME OUT WRONG

Sometimes, you'll say something that just comes out wrong, even if you didn't mean to be nasty. Apologize straightaway and, if you can, remove the post. (Not all sites allow you to do this, so sometimes an apology will have to do.)

KEEP YOUR VOICE DOWN

Online, typing in all caps can seem like you're shouting. That's fine if you're shouting "OMG CUTE PUPPIES!" but in many situations people might take it as an attack if you TALK TO THEM LIKE THIS.

STAY ON TOPIC

Don't spam: that is, don't post irrelevant things or, post the same thing over and over again. It's very annoying and might even get you banned from some sites.

Essentially, if someone's having an interesting discussion about one thing, don't assume you have the right to come in and change the subject.

GET PERMISSION

Have you got a photo of a friend of yours looking silly? Ask them before you post it.
Before you post anything about someone else, ask them if it's OK. The same goes for your parents. And they should ask permission before posting pictures of you, too.

@goofyparents
Our lovely son aged 1

SHHH, SPOILERS!

Sometimes, people don't want to read about certain topics, or know pieces of information. Say, if you're talking about a new TV show, it's polite to type 'spoiler warning' before you discuss what happens in an episode. (A spoiler is when someone gives away something from a story that you would rather have had as a surprise.)

TRIGGER WARNINGS

Some people use the phrase 'trigger warning' when they're writing about painful topics, such as discussions about violence, or mental health problems. That way people won't stumble across things that upset them.

It's called a trigger warning because reading about certain topics can trigger a very strong reaction that is painful and harmful to the person reading. Using these warnings yourself can help others to enjoy the internet safely, and when you see them, you can decide whether it's something that might be upsetting to you.

DON'T ENCOURAGE THEM

If someone's posted something cruel or really offensive, don't share it. Even if you're sharing it to say, "look how awful this is," you might be encouraging the person by giving them attention. You also risk upsetting other people who'd rather not read nasty posts.

ONE LAST CHECK

Always think before you post.

Read over what you're about to put online.

Do you really want to share that?

AND FINALLY...

... don't forget to pay attention to the people you're with in real life. It can be easy to get sucked into online life, but texting while you're paying in a shop or forever updating your status at family events is rude.

REASONS TO LOVE THE INTERNET #3
LITTLE ACTS OF KINDNESS

You have the power to put a smile on someone's face — even someone you've never met — by going out of your way to be kind online.

Try saying something kind every time you go online for the next week. (You might do this already, but doing it on purpose can really help put you in a good mood, too.) It could be as simple as thanking someone for a post, or paying them a compliment.

Have you ever put your own name into a search engine?

If you have a common one, you might find out a lot about some other 'Alex Smith'.

But you might also see all sorts of information about you, from blog posts to photos or even articles you've written for the school newspaper.

The things you post online (and the things other people post about you) make up your online reputation. You can help create a better online reputation by being careful what you post.

GOGGLER

Iyesha Lamb

Iyesha Lamb is the captain of the hockey team...

Images for Iyesha Lamb

MISTAKES THAT FOLLOW YOU

If you see things like embarrassing photos and videos, or things you wish you'd never said, you can help hide them by posting things you do want people to see, so those come up instead. If someone else has posted something untrue about you, it may be possible to get it removed from internet searches (although not from the internet).

There's information about asking search engines to take down links about you at Usborne Quicklinks (see page 138).

YOUR DIGITAL FOOTPRINT

You probably post things in lots of different places on the internet and visit a lot of sites. All the things you've posted in all those places make up your 'digital footprint'.

It's as if you're telling a rambling story about yourself, bit by bit.

A SLIGHT SNAG IN YOUR QUEST FOR WORLD DOMINATION

When you apply for jobs later in life, people might search your name online and not hire you because of what you've posted.

In the meantime, friends, teachers, parents or carers might read something that you really don't want them to see. Although the internet can feel like a private place to confess things, it really, really isn't. Some criminals have even been caught after bragging about their crimes online!

Twitting

@supercrim01 Lol just robbed a bank.

@thepolice Lol. You're under arrest.

FLOOD THE INTERNET WITH GOOD

Creating a positive online reputation isn't just about avoiding saying the wrong thing. Actively try to post good things — pictures that make people laugh, encouraging words for your friends, or reviews of books and films. Also, the more good stuff you post, the less likely it'll be that people will stumble over old mistakes you've made online.

NOT YOURS TO SHARE

Think about other people's reputations too — if you write something rude or untrue about someone else, or post an embarrassing picture of them, then you're taking away their ability to be in charge of their online reputation. It's not up to you and it's not fair.

TIDY UP BEHIND YOU

If you've stoppped using a social media site, deactivate your profile there and hide as much as you can of it. If something doesn't represent who you are right now, you might find it embarrassing if someone brings it up.

Goo Goo Ga Ga Gaming

My Profile

I love my mummywummy.com

You might want to close down accounts you used as a little kid, for example.

YOUR ALTER EGOS HAVE REPUTATIONS TOO

On sites where you don't post under your real name, reputation still matters. If you build up a positive reputation for your profile, then you'll have a more enjoyable time on the site and people will be glad to see you there. Plus, if anyone ever does make the link between the real you and this profile, it won't matter as much.

ME ME ME VS SHARING

If all your posts are about you — pictures of your glorious face for example — you could come over as quite self-centred. But if you share things about other people and talk about more interesting things than just *you you you* all the time, you'll probably get a lot more positive reactions than if you try too hard to show off.

SILENCE CAN BE GOLDEN

One of the best ways to protect your reputation online is to err on the side of not saying anything at all. You don't have to comment on every single photo or be part of every argument people are having. It's fine not to join in with drama on the internet. Not only does it mean you come off looking better, it's a lot less stressful.

REASONS TO LOVE THE INTERNET #4:
COMMUNITY

If you ever feel as though your hobbies are nerdy, or that there's something about your identity that means you don't fit in — it is almost guaranteed that the internet will show you that there are people like you out there.

CYBERBULLYING

There's always drama on the internet, and you might find people are rude to you. But online nastiness can also grow into something bigger and crueller, and become cyberbullying.

If you're on the receiving end of cyberbullying — whether in a game, by text message, or on social media — it can be very painful. But you're not alone. Everyone knows someone who's been bullied and, whenever it happens, it's awful. Understanding what cyberbullying is, why people do it, and what to do next will help you cope.

> One very important thing to remember: being cyberbullied is never your fault.

WHAT IS CYBERBULLYING?

Cyberbullying can take many forms. All of them are ugly. Cyberbullying can involve...

- Sending nasty or threatening text messages, emails or other messages in apps.

- Posting humiliating videos online.

- Setting up fake social media profiles to make fun of people or trick them into revealing personal information.

- Posting or forwarding someone else's personal information or images without their permission.

- Making abusive comments about another user on a gaming site.

- Joining in other people's rude or abusive posts or leaving racist, homophobic, transphobic or sexist comments on someone's profile page.

- Sending unwanted sexual images or sexual comments to people.

Unfortunately, creativity can be used for evil as well as good, and cyberbullies keep coming up with new ways to be horrible.

You or your friends may experience cyberbullying that's not like any of the things on the list opposite, but if the way you're being treated feels wrong, then don't ignore it. If you take action quickly, you can stop it from getting worse, or at least make yourself feel better.

STOP IT BEFORE IT STARTS

There are a few practical ways you can protect yourself from getting cyberbullied in the first place...

- Only give your phone number to people you trust and know very well in real life.

- Don't leave your phone, tablet or laptop lying around logged onto social media or other sites, as people could 'borrow' it and pretend to be you.

- Don't share your passwords with anyone, even your best friends.

- Use the highest possible privacy settings on all your social media and online gaming accounts.

IT'S NOT YOUR FAULT

When you're reading the tips in this book or anywhere else, remember one thing: it's not your responsibility to prevent cyberbullying. The people in the wrong are the bullies. Unfortunately, safety tips are not guarantees, and if they don't work, it is absolutely not your fault. Sometimes people behave in a nasty, cruel way, and that behaviour is *their* responsibility.

IT FOLLOWS YOU HOME

Some people might try to dismiss cyberbullying as less important than the stuff that happens in person. They're wrong. Cyberbullying can be worse, because you can't just go home from school and shut your door: it can be there whenever you turn on your phone or go online.

THE EFFECTS OF CYBERBULLYING

Even when you're not looking at bullying messages, the anxiety is there: who's reading cruel things about me? Who's looking at embarrassing photos of me? How can I make it all go away?

A million terrible feelings and thoughts

Brain

WHAT TO DO NEXT...

If you do experience cyberbullying, here are some suggestions of what to do next. Don't worry if what's happening to you seems mild: even

Small-scale cyberbullying can cause a lot of pain, and you should definitely take it seriously.

IF THE BULLY IS USUALLY NICE

If you're being cyberbullied by someone you've never had a problem with before, try talking to them or sending them a message. They might have posted something that they thought was funny, even if it was very much NOT funny for you. If that's the case, talk to them and ask them to delete it. This can be scary, but you might find the problem is easier to solve than you think.

If you're lucky, it might be this simple.

He said that she said that she said that he said that she said that he said that she said that he said that she said... that he said that she said that he said that

WAS IT SOMETHING I SAID?

Another possibility: the usually-nice person might think you did something to upset them, and they're getting their own back. It could be something you actually did — in which case you should apologize — or it might be a rumour someone else started about you.

Then she said that he said that he said that she said that he said that he said that she said that he said that she said...
And she said that he said that he said that she said that he said

Either way, talk to the person directly, in person — or if that sounds too hard, ask someone you're both friends with to do it for you.

If it turns out that you *did* post something that hurt their feelings, then delete any hurtful messages, apologize to them in person, then say something nice about them online, to show that you're on their team, deep down.

I'M INNOCENT!

If you didn't do anything wrong, then point out that you haven't done anything like that before, you two have always been friends, so why would you start now? Tell them you hope they can find out who did it, but it wasn't you. (And please can they delete the nasty stuff they posted in response to your fictional badness.)

BULLIES WITH A RECORD

If the bully is someone who has a history of bullying, or if it's someone you've had problems with in the past (even if it wasn't exactly bullying), then your approach has to be a bit different, and just talking to them probably won't work.

67

DRIVE-BY BULLYING

If it's a one off thing, just ignore it.
Many bullies like seeing how upset they're making
you. If you don't reply or react to their messages,
you're stopping them getting what they want.

They might just get bored
and move on. Some bullies like
to scatter insults everywhere,
and if they're not targeting you in
particular, shrugging it off can be
the easiest option.

WHAT IF IT LASTS LONGER?

When cyberbullying happens over time, then ignoring it is no use. If someone is making your life miserable, then you really need to get help from an adult, or from an older brother or sister if you have one. Speak to whoever you feel comfortable with — whether that's a parent, carer, sports coach, school counsellor or the parent of one of your friends. If you don't feel there's anyone you can bear to talk to, then call a helpline.

 You can find links to helplines on Usborne Quicklinks.

Adults aren't all powerful, and sometimes they can be unhelpful, suggesting things that won't work. Sometimes, they don't know what to do right away. Even so, it can really help to talk about it with an adult who's on your side.

CYBERBULLYING ACTION PLAN

- Make a log of all the incidents. Each time something happens, write down the date and time; what happened; how it happened and note down any evidence you have. Save any messages you've been sent or take screenshots so you can use these as evidence. (You'll find an example log on Usborne Quicklinks.)

- Block the bully and all their close friends (bullies often run in packs). If things change, you can always unblock them later..

- Check all your privacy settings are set to the highest possible security level.

- Don't discuss the bully online or in texts, as anything that might get copied and sent to them could make things worse.

- Don't answer phone calls if you don't recognize the number. Let it go to voicemail: you can use messages they leave as evidence.

- Depending on your phone network, you might be able to block the bully's number (and their friends' numbers) using your settings. There are apps to help you do this, too.

- Be extra careful about what you put online and consider sticking to private messages or instant messages with your friends for a week or so or until things die down. You're more vulnerable out in the open.

- If the bully threatens to beat you up or worse, report this to the police immediately. Making threats is a crime in many countries.

WHEN IT'S A STRANGER

Some cyberbullying happens within a school, or between people who know each other. Other bullies like to target strangers. These are sometimes known as internet trolls. One way to deal with them is to block and report them. There's an expression: "don't feed the trolls," which means, "if you don't react to them, they might get bored".

You can sometimes spot a troll before they say anything: if someone's screen name is something racist, sexist, homophobic or otherwise nasty, block them before they have a chance to strike.

HATE HATE HATE HATE!

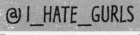
@I_HATE_GURLS

DOXXING

Internet trolls sometimes do something called 'doxxing', which means posting someone's private information online. It's meant to encourage other people to harass that person — to go to their house, for example, or telephone them. If you never post personal details online, it's easier to avoid this happening to you. If it does happen, tell an adult you trust right away so they can help you. You may want to change your phone number, if it's been posted online.

In some places, doxxing is illegal. If it happens to you, you might have to get the police involved. And, obviously, never do it yourself!

BULLIES IN GAMES

Playing games online is great fun... until someone decides to ruin it for everyone. For example, in one online building game, there are people who go around destroying things others have built, or sending them rude messages.

In most games, you can choose who you play against, or who you let into your 'world'. If in doubt, it's safest to play offline, or only accept requests from people you know and trust in real life.

IT'S GOOD TO TALK

If you're being cyberbullied (or bullied at all), the bad feelings can seem overwhelming. It's not always possible to stop cyberbullying, especially if it's anonymous, so you don't know who's targeting you. It can just be a matter of finding ways to cope until it stops.

Talking helps!

Taking care of yourself is very important and talking about your feelings can help. If you don't feel comfortable talking to people in your life, there are some great helplines for young people.

 There's a list of helplines on Usborne Quicklinks. Some of them are open 24 hours a day.

WHY DOES TALKING HELP?

It might not be obvious why talking about your feelings is helpful, when it doesn't stop the bad thing that's happening to you. Why *does* it help? And who should you talk to?

- Bottling up feelings can make them worse, because you feel alone with them. Sharing your feelings reminds you that people are there for you.

- Talking to someone can help you see your situation from a new perspective.

- If you're dealing with bad feelings on your own, it can be easy to feel that you're exaggerating or being overdramatic. Having someone listen to you helps you take your own feelings seriously.

- You could confide in a close friend, an adult you trust, or call a helpline. You could also go and talk to a school counsellor — someone who's trained to listen and help people deal with difficult feelings.

COPING WITH ANGER (AND OTHER BAD FEELINGS)

If you're being cyberbullied, it's natural to feel angry. Anger can be a useful way of coping, because it stops you from feeling weak or defeated. That anger has to go somewhere, though...

Here are a few ways to use your anger positively, so you don't have to take it out on the people in your life:

Exercise: kickboxing, punching pillows, running outside, dancing, swimming or anything that gets the blood pumping and muscles working releases chemicals that help to calm you.

Creativity: writing stories, drawing, even just scribbling black lines all over a journal is a great way to channel your frustration.

Keep a journal: write down your feelings. You could even just write angry words all over the page.

Use your imagination: there's a technique called visualization that you can use. Picture your bad thoughts as clouds in the sky and imagine them floating away. (It can take some practice.)

Focus on your strengths: doing activities that you're good at can help you feel better about yourself.

Reach out to other people who are being bullied: knowing that there are other people in the same boat can remind you that you're not alone, and there's nothing wrong with you.

WHEN THE FEELINGS GET BAD

Some people find that feeling bad leads them to have urges to hurt, or even kill, themselves. If you ever feel like this, please, please talk to someone. You are valuable and you deserve to be safe and happy.

STAY SAFE

This is the most important thing to remember... However bad you feel, there is always a way out that doesn't involve hurting yourself.

YOU ARE NOT TO BLAME

You might think you've done something to deserve being bullied. That isn't true. If someone is sending you hateful messages or spreading lies about you online, that says a lot more about them than it does about you. Bullying is wrong, but it doesn't mean there's something wrong with you.

Beautiful people get bullied

SPORTY PEOPLE GET BULLIED

Funny people get bullied

Kind people get bullied

Thin people get bullied

Famous people get bullied

TALL PEOPLE GET BULLIED

CLEVER PEOPLE GET BULLIED

Short people get bullied

POPULAR PEOPLE GET BULLIED

WHY DO PEOPLE CYBERBULLY?

There are lots of reasons, but people who cyberbully often do it because:

- They are jealous of you.

- They get pleasure out of making people feel bad.

- They want to feel powerful.

- They are trying to hide from bad things in their own lives (such as feeling insecure about how they look, or about not having a happy home life).

None of those reasons justifies bullying, but it can help to remember that your bullies are just human beings with their own fears. They're not *really* powerful; they're weak.

COULD YOU BE A CYBERBULLY?

Not all villains wear black hats and cloaks and twirl their evil moustaches. Sometimes, you can find yourself doing cruel things without realizing it. Perhaps you're feeling bad about something and you start taking it out on someone else? Or you make fun of someone for a joke, and it gets out of hand?

Even joining in when someone else is sending cruel messages is cyberbullying. If you forward a bullying message, that's still bullying. If you forward an image that's sexual, or a message that contains a violent threat, you could even be convicted of a crime.

It's not hard to avoid this kind of thing: you just need to think carefully about what you say and do online.

HELPING YOUR FRIENDS

If your friends are being cyberbullied, you can help them by talking to them about how they're feeling. If they're being cyberbullied by someone at your school, and you know who's doing it, you could join together with other friends to confront the bully. (Only do this if you feel safe doing it.) Encourage your friends to talk to an adult, too.

84

VIOLENT THREATS AND STALKING

Some bullying is a crime. If someone is sending you violent threats, or obsessively sending you messages, talk to an adult about contacting the police. This is where keeping a log of the messages you've received is really important. Think of yourself as a detective: you need all that evidence to catch your criminal.

However, it's not your responsibility to make sure the person stalking you or sending you violent threats is punished. That's the police's job.

REASONS TO LOVE THE INTERNET #5:
COOL, LOVELY, RANDOM THINGS

This chapter has had some upsetting things in it.
Do an image or video search for some of these things
to balance out the darkness:

Rocket launch videos

Robot football tournament

Extreme skateboard stunts

Baby turtle

Kittens

World Beard and Moustache Championships®

Aurora Borealis (or Northern Lights)

Tardigrades (they are amazing, tiny creatures)

WHO OWNS IDEAS?
(AND HOW TO AVOID A VISIT FROM THE POLICE)

6

People post their creations online all the time, whether it's musicians uploading their songs, or someone writing fanfiction* about their favourite TV show.

Sometimes, copying or stealing the content people put online can get you into a lot of trouble. Sometimes, it's just rude. Either way, it's important to avoid taking things you aren't supposed to have.

There are no special internet police who arrive with flashing siren gifs when someone steals or misbehaves online. But you might get a scary call from a real-life lawyer if you use or share content that isn't yours.

> What's illegal online varies depending on where you live. But violent threats are usually illegal.

*In case you haven't already come across this glorious thing, fanfiction (or fanfic) = stories people write online about their favourite books, TV shows, movies and so on, playing with existing characters and taking them on new adventures.

YAY, FREE MUSIC!

Everyone loves getting things for free, and there are quite a few ways to listen to music online without paying — such as services that allow you to stream music in return for listening to some adverts.

However, some of the free stuff you might find online could get you in trouble.

Downloading something that someone else owns and hasn't given permission for people to share online is illegal in some countries.

COPYRIGHT

Copyright is a legal term that means the creator (or sometimes the owner) of a work has the right to say what people can do with it. If you have the copyright in something, then you get to decide if people can make copies of it, put it online and so on. Some things aren't copyrighted — for example, books that were written about 100 years ago — but it's always safest to assume something is in copyright.

NOT ALL PIRATES HAVE PARROTS

I'm a terrible person in a wonderful hat.

HELP!

Illegally downloading a copyrighted thing from the internet, or sharing a copyrighted file, such as a video, is often called piracy. That makes it sound exciting, but it's basically stealing. (Old-fashioned pirates were just thieves with big boats and fancy hats, after all.)

File sharing or downloading from the internet isn't illegal in itself: if someone has put something online that they have permission to share, it's OK to download it.

THE DOWNSIDES OF DOWNLOADS

Illegal downloading can get you (or your parents) into trouble with the law. It can also mean your computer gets a virus. Some computer viruses can be so destructive that anti-virus software won't help, and you'll have to get a new computer, or at least take it to a shop for some serious mending.

(This could mean a very awkward conversation when you have to ask for money to fix your computer.)

How did you get the virus?

Erm... my hand slipped and I accidentally downloaded 22 episodes of Dragon War?

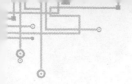
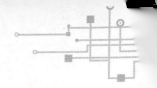

AM I BREAKING THE LAW?

The law varies from place to place, but here are a few things that are against the law to share online in a lot of places:

- Copyrighted material such as videos, songs, stories and films.

- Sexual images of underage children (that could include pictures of people you know, so think before you forward a rude picture that's going around your school).

- Threatening posts or messages saying that you're going to harm someone.

WHAT WILL HAPPEN TO ME?

Again, punishments vary from place to place. You might get a warning for doing something like illegally downloading, or your parents might get a fine. For more serious online crimes, your punishment could be worse.

PIRACY HURTS ARTISTS

Some people try to defend online piracy by saying that it doesn't hurt anyone. It's not like stealing someone's bag, where if you take their bag, they don't have it any more: with someone's digital property, they still have it if you copy it.

What they *do* lose out on is the ability to make a living from the thing they've made.

If you're in a band and you want to sell your music, people are less likely to want to give you money for it if someone else is giving it away (illegally) for free.

That's not just sad for the creator: not making money from music might mean they can't afford to be a musician any more, so their fans end up losing out too. There are lots of services where you can get your music (or any other kind of entertainment you get online) legally. It can mean you have a better chance of hearing more from the artists you love in the future.

GIVING CREDIT

Even if someone is sharing their work online for free, it's a good habit always to say where you found a piece of work and give a credit to the creator.

93

HOMEWORK HELP

It's not illegal to cheat on your homework but it can still get you into trouble if your teacher notices that your work sounds suspiciously like a Wikipedia article.

It's fine to use quotations (words other people have said) as long as you make it clear you're quoting someone else, and never just copy out chunks of information you found online as though they're yours.

Copying from the internet means you not only risk detention, but teacher sarcasm. Not to mention potentially failing your exams.

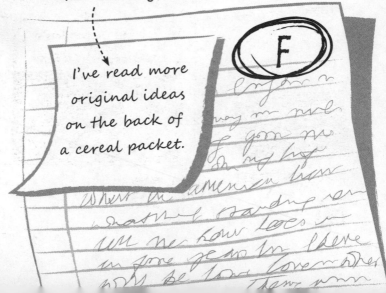

I've read more original ideas on the back of a cereal packet.

FINDING FACTS NOT NONSENSE

Anyone can post their ideas online. This is great when it comes to being able to express yourself. On the downside, it means a lot of what you read online is nonsense, whether that's made-up 'facts' or badly thought-out opinions.

When you're researching online, try to cross-check information you find against other websites. Think about the type of information you're looking for: if you want to find information for an art project, for example, a reliable place to try might be the website for a famous museum or art gallery.

REASONS TO LOVE THE INTERNET #6:
MAKING AND SHARING YOUR OWN STUFF

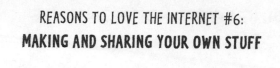

Platforms like YouTube™
allow you to share your talents
with the world. Some vloggers
(people who make and share videos,
usually about their lives or hobbies) end
up with huge followings and get paid for what
they do. If you're camera-shy, you can
share your artwork, your music,
or your coding knowledge.

NOTE: sharing things you've made
online does leave you open to copying,
but the satisfaction you can get from
people enjoying your amazing ideas often
outweighs that risk.

SPENDING MONEY

7

The internet itself is free, and there are many apps and sites out there that you don't have to pay to use. Still, it's easy to find yourself spending a lot of money online without meaning to.

If you have access to a credit card or bankcard — or you know the login details to sites where the adults in your life store their card details — then you could end up with huge bills.

There's something about clicking on a purchase that makes it feel as though it's not real money. But don't let that feeling fool you.

IN-APP PURCHASES

A lot of free games aren't free when you look closely. You might find that you're asked to pay in order to access more levels, characters or other objects in the game, such as fancy weapons.

If you have access to money online, it's easy to end up spending far more than you realize. One option: you could ask for a prepaid card with a set amount of money, so you can never spend more than they want you to. Or stick to games that are genuinely free.

Ask *every* time whether it's ok to buy something online using your parent or guardian's bankcard — even if they've given you permission to use a particular card before.

ONLINE GAMBLING

When people talk about addiction, they are often thinking about drugs or alcohol. Gambling is an addiction that people talk less about, even though it can cause a lot of harm.

When you're underage, you're not legally allowed to gamble, so if you do, you're breaking the law.

Are you over 18?

If you're ever tempted, it's worth remembering that gambling doesn't just put you at risk of huge debts (for you or your parents or carers), it's also emotionally damaging, as it gives you a short-term rush that you can't sustain without gambling more. Basically, it's a very expensive way to cause yourself pain.

If you're worried that you might have a problem with gambling, you can find information about getting help and support on Quicklinks.

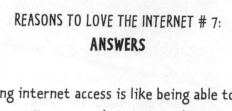

REASONS TO LOVE THE INTERNET # 7:
ANSWERS

Having internet access is like being able to tap
into a million people's brains. Can't remember
the name of an actor? Need to know how much
the average cow weighs? What's the capital of
Russia? You are seconds away from knowing.
(For tips on how to find *reliable* information,
go to Usborne Quicklinks.)

Spend long enough on the internet, and you're likely to see something sexual — whether it's a picture, or just someone talking about sex. Adults may try to set up computer filters (programs that stop certain things appearing in searches, for example) but things always slip through the net.

You may feel ready to read about sex, you may not. Either way, you need to know how to navigate the internet when it comes to sexual images, and protect yourself emotionally (and even legally).

 THIS PAGE IS NSFW

That means Not Safe For Work. That is, it's something you wouldn't want your boss to see on your screen if you were an adult. Some NSFW pages might upset or disturb you, so approach with caution.

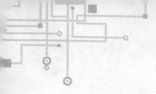

PORN

There are images and videos on the internet of naked people in sexual poses, or having sex (often both). This is known as pornography, or porn. Even if you don't seek these out, you might stumble across them.

Not all nudity you'll see online is pornography — porn is designed to give people sexual feelings. However, it can be a blurry line.

I'm not porn. I'm art. Unless I'm very old-fashioned porn?

ARE YOU OK?

Whether or not something's technically porn doesn't matter too much. What matters is you. If you see anything that makes you feel uncomfortable, or upset, just shut the browser.

Even if all your friends are looking at it, your feelings are what matter. If you don't want to look at a picture, or a video, that is totally up to you.

It might be something you'll be interested in later on, or might never be your thing. One of the most important lessons you can ever learn about sex is that it's always, *always* ok to say no — whether it's to actions or images.

> Your feelings and decisions matter.
> Don't ever let anyone else tell you that you
> *should* feel ready for something that makes
> you uncomfortable. It's always your choice.

THE LAW'S THERE FOR YOU

Laws about porn vary from country to country, but usually there are age limits, meaning you're not allowed to see or watch porn when you're underage. (For example, you have to be 18 in the UK.) While you're unlikely to be arrested for viewing porn, it's worth asking yourself *why* it's against the law.

The law is there to protect young people. It's not necessarily that seeing pictures of people having sex will scar you for life, but it might be very upsetting, especially because the sex in porn can give you some unrealistic and damaging ideas of what sex is, and what bodies should look like.

I don't look like her...

Ew! I don't think I ever want to do THAT.

IT'S ALL A PERFORMANCE

Like in any film, porn is acting — bad acting, maybe, but it's not real sex. If you watch porn before you've had sex, you might end up with the impression that you should be doing all kinds of things you're not comfortable with.

Always remember, if you see porn, that it is not what you're 'meant' to do when you have sex. It's as made-up and fake as an advert.

EVERY BODY IS DIFFERENT

Your body is yours, and what you do with it is up to you. Porn stars may have fake breasts, or shave off all their pubic hair. Seeing bodies like this can make people feel that there's something wrong with their own bodies.

It can also give you strange ideas about what your partner's body should look like.

But there is no one way you *should* look. Everyone is different in real life, and that is absolutely fine.

Some people look at porn and enjoy it, and that's perfectly OK. Other people can develop an unhealthy addiction, and start to feel they need it. If you feel worried about using porn too much, you can find information about how to ask for help on Usborne Quicklinks.

SEXTING

Sending pictures of yourself with no (or few) clothes on is sometimes called sexting. This is something to be very cautious about. Even if you're sending it to a girlfriend or boyfriend, and you trust them with your life, it's very easy for pictures to spread beyond the person you texted them to. You're just a few slips of the thumb away from going viral without your pants on.

REVENGE PORN

Pictures don't always get shared by accident, or even "just for a joke". When someone shares naked pictures of an ex-boyfriend or ex-girlfriend in order to embarrass them, that's known as revenge porn. This is one reason why it's safest to avoid sending any pictures that you're not comfortable showing to the world.

OTHER PEOPLE'S PHOTOS

If you ever get sent naked photos, do NOT send them on to anyone else, whatever you do. It's not just cruel; it might also be illegal.

Sharing images of children (anyone under 18 in most countries) can mean you're guilty of distributing child abuse images, even if it's a picture of one of your mates.

This is a very serious crime, and you definitely don't want it going on your record.

WORDS, WORDS, WORDS

Not all sexual messages have pictures in them. That doesn't mean it's a good idea to fire off texts full of rude suggestions. Just like pictures, text messages can fall into the wrong hands. Sexual text messages can leave you feeling vulnerable, especially if you don't get a positive reaction.

QUESTIONS TO ASK BEFORE YOU SEND A SEXT...

• How would you feel if everyone in school saw it? Or if your parents saw it? The police?

• Are you sending it because you really want to, or because other people do it?

• Is there a safer way to tell someone that you like them?

• How are you going to feel the moment after you press send?

SEX AND SELF-ESTEEM

As you get older, you may find that you start worrying about whether or not people find you attractive. (If you don't, brilliant, you're lucky.)

The internet can make the worry worse: feeling as though everyone else is better-looking than you is easy when people only post the most flattering pictures of themselves.

This is your insecurity.

This is your insecurity online.

Just as with porn, remember: images are not reality, and your worth as a human being has nothing to do with whether or not lots of people say you look good in a photograph. (Or in real life, for that matter.)

GETTING ANSWERS AND SUPPORT
The internet can be a great resource to find answers to embarrassing questions about sex and relationships. On Usborne Quicklinks, you'll find links to sites with helpful information about sex and all the worries that go with it.

REASONS TO LOVE THE INTERNET #8:
INSPIRATION

Whether you're arty, sporty or into science,
you can find inspiration on the internet.
You can find videos online that teach you how
to write computer code, how to create
different effects in your artwork, how to
score a goal in soccer, or even how to create
your own YouTube™ videos.

Before you read this chapter, it's worth remembering that the adults it's talking about aren't typical. The world isn't full of monsters who want to hurt you.

Unfortunately, there *are* some bad people out there. This chapter will help you protect yourself against them. Some of it might be upsetting, so you could always get a parent or carer to read it first and then talk to them about it.

ONLINE PREDATORS

There are, unfortunately, adults out there who want to hurt children and young people. Some of them want to touch or talk to young people in a sexual way, which is illegal and very harmful. This is known as sexual abuse, or child sexual exploitation, and the adults who do it are often called sexual predators or paedophiles. Adults may use all kinds of trickery to get to know children.

GROOMING

You don't always know who you're talking to online, and predators often pretend to be children themselves. They try to gain a young person's trust, in order to get close to them. This is known as grooming.

SOME WARNING SIGNS

Watch out for someone who...

⚠️ ...flatters you or really sucks up to you. They might be trying to make you feel special to gain your trust.

⚠️ ...tells you dirty jokes or changes the subject to something sexual.

⚠️ ...asks you personal questions, especially about your body.

⚠️ ...tells you not to mention a conversation to anyone else, or asks you to keep secrets.

⚠️ ...mirrors your opinions and interests. Predators often pretend to like the same things as you.

⚠️ ...tells you that you can't trust your family.

⚠️ ... says they want to be your boyfriend or girlfriend, even though you've never met.

Tell a trusted adult if anyone you talk to online does any of these things. If you don't have an adult you feel comfortable talking to, you can find links to helplines and websites on Usborne Quicklinks. (See page 138.)

PROTECTING YOURSELF

There are many reasons to avoid giving away too much personal information online. But one important one is to protect yourself from predators.

If a predator can build up a picture of you, including where you live and places you often visit, they could come to find you.

> **YOU:** My local pool is amazing! It's got this insane waterslide!

> **THEM:**
> Oh, where's that? I'd love to go.

> **YOU:** In Oxley, do u live near there?

> **THEM:** LOL I do! Do you go on Saturday mornings...maybe see u there?

Predators could also use information they've learned about you to gain your trust and create a false sense of close friendship.

IT'S NOT JUST STRANGERS

Online abuse can also involve people you already know, such as adults you might meet at a party or a school event.

By using the internet to talk to you, a predator who you know in real life can contact you while you're alone, without anyone else — such as parents, carers or teachers — knowing.

If you receive messages from adults you know, even if the messages seem harmless, show them to a parent or carer. It's best that they know if adults are trying to talk to you online, so they can help to keep you safe.

Whether or not you already know the adult you're talking to, if they ask to meet up alone in real life (IRL)... DON'T.

DIGITAL ABUSE

Not all predators ask to meet in real life. It can still be abuse if it all remains digital. For example, they might ask for photos of you naked, or send you photos of them. They might also try to start sexual conversations. Even if you never meet them and they never touch you, this is still very wrong of them.

THE DANGERS OF WEBCAMS

If someone asks you to talk with them on a webcam, say no. A predator might want to trick you into showing them parts of your body, or to make you pose in sexual ways on camera.

Super creepy fact: webcams can be hacked, so close your computer when you're not using it, as someone who's hacked into your webcam could use it to spy on you.

Some webcams look like this

The camera on a tablet or laptop is often very small

WHAT TO DO IF YOU'RE ABUSED

If you suffer abuse (whether it's online or offline or both), it's important to tell someone, talk about your feelings and get help. Even if you haven't had any physical contact with the predator, abuse can have a very powerful and upsetting impact on you.

Remember: none of this is your fault, and it's normal to have all kinds of confusing feelings about it. The person who abused you is a criminal, so you can get your parents or carers to report them to the police.

Although it will be painful, keep a record of any abusive messages or inappropriate images or videos. This will help the police to prove that the abuser has committed a crime, and punish them.

There is advice on Usborne Quicklinks for parents and carers about how to support young people who've been abused. (See page 138.)

VERY BAD IDEAS

Some harmful adults on the internet aren't there to abuse young people sexually. Instead, they use the internet to reach out to young people to try to mould their minds. Some go even further, trying to persuade children and teenagers to commit crimes.

Terrorists, for example, use the internet to try to persuade young people to plant bombs or carry out other violent acts.

Just like sexual predators, people like this often use tactics such as flattery, to make you feel special. They may try to persuade you that helping them is the best way to give your life meaning — that joining them will make you a hero...

...when actually they want to turn you into a murderer.

HOW TO SPOT THIS

If someone on the internet posts about committing violent acts, the alarm bells should start to ring. They might not be this obvious, though. Some may start by asking you questions about right and wrong, and talking about all the things that are wrong with the world today.

Not everyone who's angry on the internet is trying to make you believe harmful things. But, if someone's comments go further than just moaning — if they start to say that a certain group of people is evil and deserves to be hurt, it's time to step away.

If someone online is trying to persuade you to do something dangerous, or even just to *believe* hateful or violent ideas, tell an adult you trust. If you don't have someone to talk to, there are helplines listed on Usborne Quicklinks.

Stories

You can find some amazing stories on the internet, from webcomics to classic fairytales to fanfiction.

For example, all the fairytales told by the Brothers Grimm are available for free online. (You might discover that they're a bit nastier than the versions you might have seen as cartoons when you were little.)

If you're being bullied or having other serious problems online, you don't have to deal with it on your own.

This chapter gives some suggestions about how to ask for help for some of the problems you might have online. (There's a section at the back of the book for adults, giving them tips on how they can help you, too, as well as lots of links on the Usborne Quicklinks website.)

I'm here.

How can I help?

NO PROBLEM TOO SMALL

It can be hard to tell people that you're having problems. Sometimes you might feel embarrassed, or that your problems are your fault. You might feel that it's not that serious and you should be able to cope alone. Sometimes, you might feel it's not a real problem if it's happening on the internet and not in 'real life.'

> Don't be so sensitive, it's just internet drama, shrug it off.

But if something is making you feel sad or uncomfortable, it's a real problem, and you deserve to have help.

Unhelpful inner voice

> Your feelings matter. Ask for help.

Helpful inner voice

WHO TO ASK FOR HELP

- **Friends:** if you're being cyberbullied, talking things through with your friends can really help.

- **Parents, guardians or carers:** it's their job to listen to you and help you solve your problems. They can also help you work out if someone you're talking to online might be dangerous.

- **Telephone helplines or online help services:** it can be hard to talk about very personal problems. If you don't feel there's anyone in your life you can talk to, there are helplines that are anonymous. (There are suggestions on Usborne Quicklinks.)

- **School counsellor or doctor:** if you're feeling stressed or overwhelmed, ask your parent, guardian or teacher to make you an appointment with a doctor or a counsellor at your school.

- **Social media:** most social media and websites have help pages on how to report problems, as well as delete posts or pictures.

BE REALISTIC

Some people will be better at helping you with the emotional side of things than with anything technical. Your parents or carers might not be as confident using the internet as you are, but they can be there for you as a shoulder to cry on, and they can help you with things such as getting the police involved if the situation is very serious.

We love you and support you always. But we're not quite sure how the Youthy Tubes work...

If you want help with the more technical side of things, you could ask a teacher you trust, who's good at computers.

If you're struggling, you're not alone, and it's nothing to be ashamed of. About two thirds of all young people in the United Kingdom alone experience cyberbullying. For about a quarter of those young people, the bullying happens often.

FEELINGS ARE NOT FOREVER

Online abuse of any kind is horrible. It can make you feel very lonely, scared and even ashamed. All these feelings are normal. Talk to people about how you feel — and remember, feelings don't last forever. You will feel better. In the long run, everything will be ok.

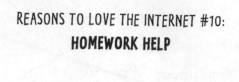

REASONS TO LOVE THE INTERNET #10:
HOMEWORK HELP

Copying your homework off Wikipedia is a bad
move, but there are a lot of sites that you can
use to help you do research and find interesting
facts to include in your homework, or in
school projects.

The key to using the internet for homework
is to make sure you use trusted sites, written
or checked by experts, and to try to use lots
of different sources and write it in your own
words, rather than copying out long chunks
from a single place.

DIGITAL DETOX

With all its faults, the internet is amazing. But sometimes, *no* internet can be great too.

From time to time, if you turn off your phone, put away the tablet and shut down the computer, it can be great for your mood, for your body, and for your friendships. The internet is not the only place in the world. Give yourself permission to take a break and get offline.

INFORMATION OVERLOAD

On the internet, you're bombarded with information: words, pictures, adverts, videos and the rest. It can make you feel really burned out and overwhelmed, even if no one's being unpleasant to you.

If you factor in bullying and other bad things that can happen, the internet can get utterly exhausting. Your brain needs a break.

If I have to look at another advert for fad diets I am going to jump out of your skull and run away to a desert island.

Avoid your brain going on strike by taking time out.

FEAR OF MISSING OUT

Taking a break from the internet and social media can seem scary.

Don't overestimate how important the internet is. Sending a picture of yourself with a filter that makes you look like a dog can wait a few days.

From time to time, give yourself a break. You can tell your friends you won't be online for a while if you're worried about just disappearing.

GET OUTSIDE

When you spend a lot of time online (most people do), it's easy to forget that the world beyond the internet is rather beautiful.

Spending time outdoors is good for you, too. And sure, "It's good for you" is not a reason that convinces many people to do stuff. But here's the thing: it's also really enjoyable. Natural light and exercise put you in a better mood — plus you need some sun on your skin to produce Vitamin D, which helps your body protect your bones, teeth and muscles.

What is this strange, warm yellow light hitting my face?

CONVERSATIONS IN THE FLESH

Talking to people, face to face, where you can see their expressions and hear them laugh, is another way to make yourself feel good.

There's also the fact that when you step away from social media, you can see someone as a whole person, flaws and all, and not the polished, edited version of themselves they present online.

YOU'RE NOT JUST A MIND

Being online can make you feel very stuck inside your own head. Take time to connect with your body, too.

Go for a run or a swim, play a sport you like (whether or not you're any good)... any of these things can remind you that it feels good to move more than just your thumbs or your mouse-clicking finger.

IT WILL ALL BE OK

The internet can be wonderful, as long as you a) spend plenty of time OFF it, b) remember that it's just a tool and c) take care. Be wary, take precautions, and you can still have an amazing time online. The internet is a mixed bag of good and bad, fun and danger. Just like the world, really.

REASONS TO LOVE THE INTERNET #11:
IT GIVES YOU IDEAS OF THINGS TO DO *OFFLINE*

If you're ever sitting around the house and bored, you can find inspiration online for places to go and things to see. For example...

- Museums and art galleries

- Skate parks or natural spaces with soothing sounds of tweeting birds and babbling brooks

- Historical sites, from Ancient Roman ruins to castles where you can try on armour

- Amusement parks and other places with rides that make you scream your face off

- City sights and hidden places you might pass every day without noticing

USBORNE QUICKLINKS

The internet is a great source of information about online safety, but it's important to know where to look and what to believe.

We have selected some useful websites to help you stay safe online, or find support if you're receiving abusive messages or having other difficulties. At Usborne Quicklinks you'll find links to websites and helplines that provide support to young people being bullied or abused online. To balance out the negative, we've added some more fun websites with video clips and activities that help you get the most out of the internet.

For links to all these sites go to:
www.usborne.com/quicklinks
and enter the keywords "staying safe online"

TIPS FOR PARENTS, CARERS AND OTHER GROWN-UPS

The internet is now a normal part of growing up, but it can be worrying as a parent, knowing that your children could be coming across all kinds of harmful material (and people) online.

KEEPING THEM SAFE

Talking to your children, or the young people in your care, about where they go and who they talk to online is very important. Knowing about the sites they visit and the apps they use gives you more power — it's especially important to make sure you understand privacy settings, as well as how to block and report people who send abusive messages. You can find out how to do this in the help section of each app or site.

Who are you chatting to?

What app is that?

GETTING HELP

If your child has had very bad experiences online, or is being abused or cyberbullied, there are various online support services and phone helplines (you'll find links on Usborne Quicklinks, see page 138). It's also worth finding out if your child's school has a counsellor, or talk to your doctor about getting a referral to a therapist.

Children may feel that bullying or abuse is their fault, so make sure you reassure them that it's not, and encourage them to talk about it.

REPORTING ABUSE

If your child experiences harassment online, or worse abuse, this may be a crime. If you're in doubt, discuss it with your local police, or try one of the helplines listed on the Usborne Quicklinks site.

INDEX